W9-BAR-130

MATH PRACTICE

New York • Toronto • London • Auckland • Sydney
Mexico City • New Delhi • Hong Kong • Buenos Aires

Teaching *Resources*

Cover design by Jay Namerow
Interior illustrations by Teresa Anderko, Jon Buller, Reggie Holladay, Anne Kennedy, Bob Masheris, Mark Mason, and Carol Tiernon
Interior design by Quack & Company

ISBN 0-439-81916-4

1 2 3 4 5 6 7 8 9 10   40   13 12 11 10 09 08 07 06

Table of Contents

Dear Parent:

Welcome to *2nd Grade Math Practice!* This valuable tool is designed to help your child succeed in school. Scholastic, the most trusted name in learning, has been creating quality educational materials for school and home for nearly a century. And this resource is no exception.

Inside this book, you'll find colorful and engaging activity pages that will give your child the practice he or she needs to master essential skills, such as adding and subtracting, identifying shapes and patterns, telling time, measuring, and so much more.

To support your child's learning experience at home, try these helpful tips:

- Provide a comfortable, well-lit place to work, making sure your child has all the supplies he or she needs.

- Encourage your child to work at his or her own pace. Children learn at different rates and will naturally develop skills in their own time.

- Praise your child's efforts. If your child makes a mistake, offer words of encouragement and positive help.

- Display your child's work and celebrate his successes with family and friends.

We hope you and your child will enjoy working together to complete this workbook.

Happy learning!
The Editors

Order Recorder

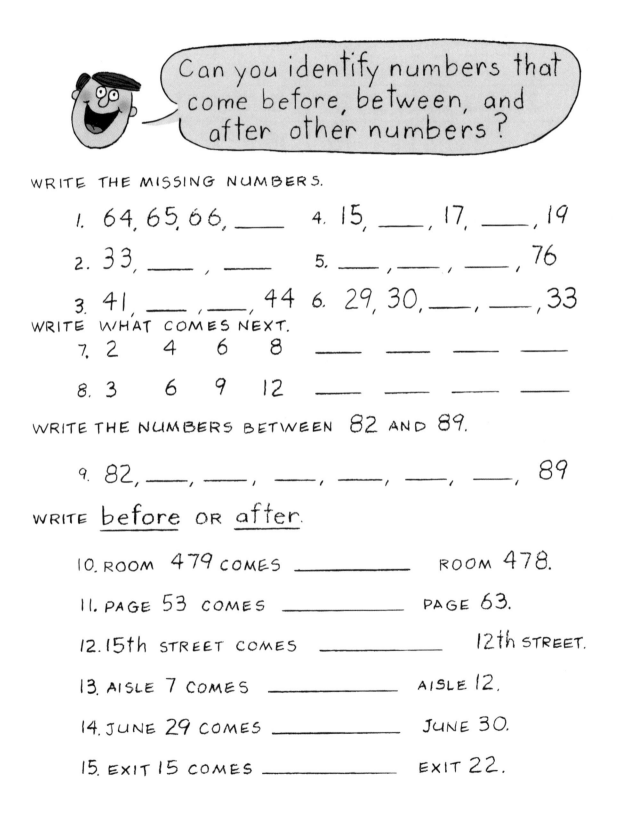

Can you identify numbers that come before, between, and after other numbers?

WRITE THE MISSING NUMBERS.

1. 64, 65, 66, ____

2. 33, ____ , ____

3. 41, ____ , ____ , 44

4. 15, ____ , 17, ____ , 19

5. ____ , ____ , ____ , 76

6. 29, 30, ____ , ____ , 33

WRITE WHAT COMES NEXT.

7. 2   4   6   8   ___   ___   ___   ___

8. 3   6   9   12   ___   ___   ___   ___

WRITE THE NUMBERS BETWEEN 82 AND 89.

9. 82, ____ , ____ , ____ , ____ , ____ , ____ , 89

WRITE before OR after.

10. ROOM 479 COMES _____ ROOM 478.

11. PAGE 53 COMES _____ PAGE 63.

12. 15th STREET COMES _____ 12th STREET.

13. AISLE 7 COMES _____ AISLE 12.

14. JUNE 29 COMES _____ JUNE 30.

15. EXIT 15 COMES _____ EXIT 22.

Picking Out Patterns

On the 100th day of school, everyone in Pat's class picked out patterns on the 100 Chart. Look at the chart below.

1	2	3	4	5	6	7	8	9	10
11	12	13	14	15	16	17	18	19	20
21	22	23	24	25	26	27	28	29	30
31	32	33	34	35	36	37	38	39	40
41	42	43	44	45	46	47	48	49	50
51	52	53	54	55	56	57	58	59	60
61	62	63	64	65	66	67	68	69	70
71	72	73	74	75	76	77	78	79	80
81	82	83	84	85	86	87	88	89	90
91	92	93	94	95	96	97	98	99	100

1. Find and finish the pattern starting with 2, 12, 22.

_____

2. Find and finish the pattern starting with 100, 90, 80.

_____

3. Find and finish the pattern starting with 97, 87, 77.

_____

4. Find and finish the pattern starting with 11, 22, 33.

_____

Amused Chooser

Compare numbers: > means greater than. < means less than. = means same as. Hint: The arrow points to the number that is less.

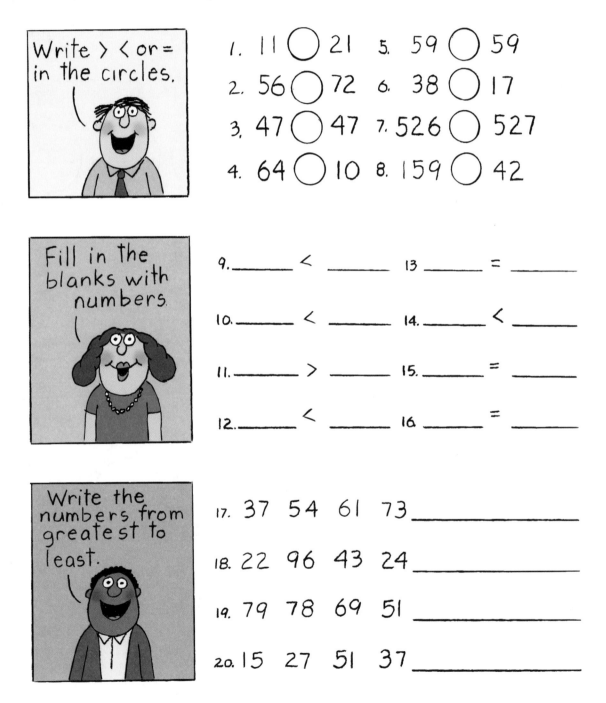

Write > < or = in the circles.

1. 11 ◯ 21   5. 59 ◯ 59
2. 56 ◯ 72   6. 38 ◯ 17
3. 47 ◯ 47   7. 526 ◯ 527
4. 64 ◯ 10   8. 159 ◯ 42

Fill in the blanks with numbers.

9. _____ < _____   13 _____ = _____

10. _____ < _____   14. _____ < _____

11. _____ > _____   15. _____ = _____

12. _____ < _____   16. _____ = _____

Write the numbers from greatest to least.

17. 37 54 61 73 _____

18. 22 96 43 24 _____

19. 79 78 69 51 _____

20. 15 27 51 37 _____

Coin-Toss Addition

Toss 8 coins. Write "**H**" for heads or "**T**" for tails in the circles below to show your toss. Then write the addition equation. Write the number of "heads" first. We did the first one for you. Try it three times.

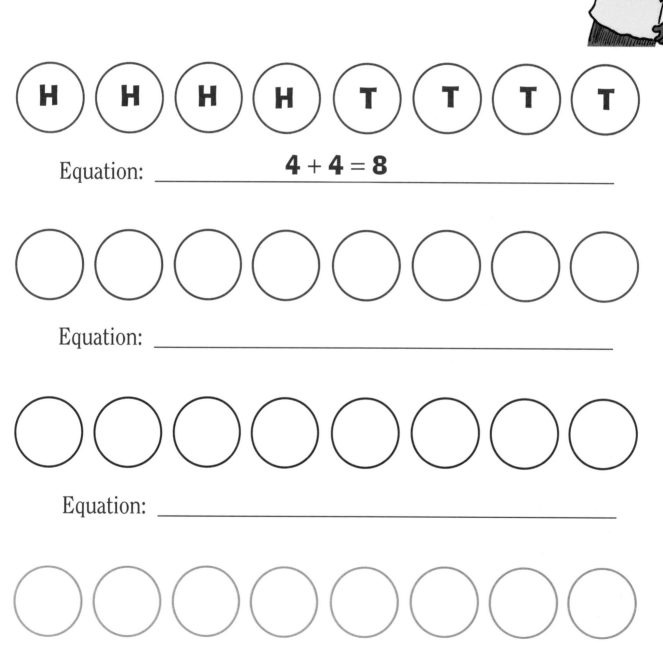

(H) (H) (H) (H) (T) (T) (T) (T)

Equation: _____ **4 + 4 = 8** _____

( ) ( ) ( ) ( ) ( ) ( ) ( ) ( )

Equation: _____

( ) ( ) ( ) ( ) ( ) ( ) ( ) ( )

Equation: _____

( ) ( ) ( ) ( ) ( ) ( ) ( ) ( )

Equation: _____

Time to Get Up!

Twenty animals were hibernating near Sleepy Pond.
5 of them woke up. Color 5 animals below.

How many are still sleeping? _____

A week later, 7 more woke up. Color 7 other animals.

How many are still sleeping? _____

Spell It Out

Add. Complete the puzzle using number words.

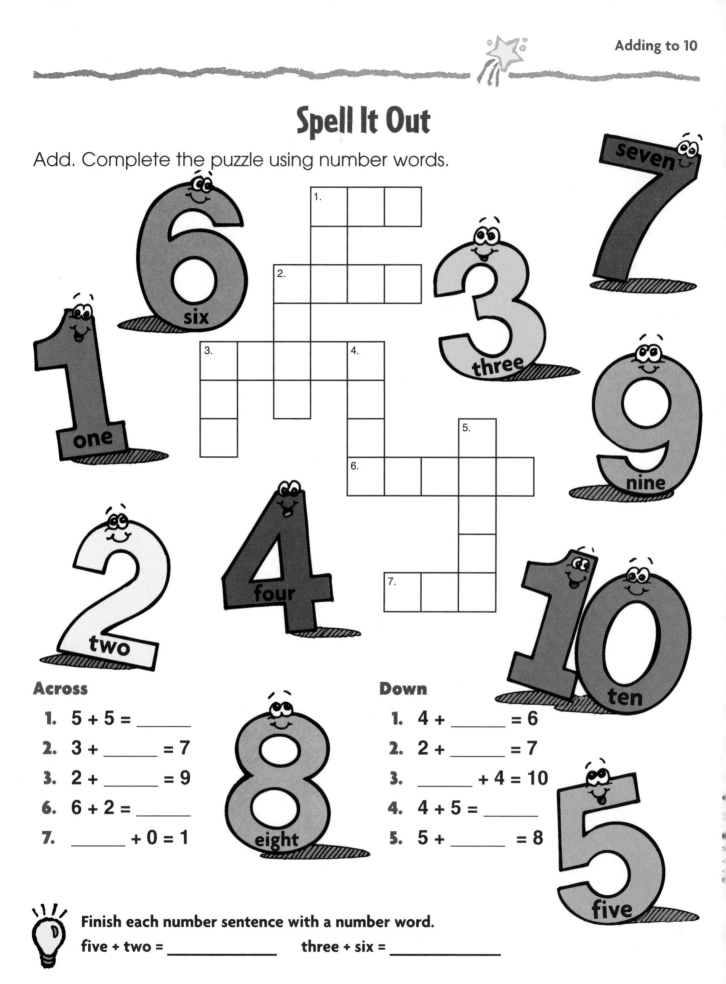

Across

1. $5 + 5 =$ _____
2. $3 +$ _____ $= 7$
3. $2 +$ _____ $= 9$
6. $6 + 2 =$ _____
7. _____ $+ 0 = 1$

Down

1. $4 +$ _____ $= 6$
2. $2 +$ _____ $= 7$
3. _____ $+ 4 = 10$
4. $4 + 5 =$ _____
5. $5 +$ _____ $= 8$

Finish each number sentence with a number word.

five + two = _____   three + six = _____

Beautiful Bouquets

Subtract. Draw petals to show the difference.

Color the bows with an even number yellow.
Color the bows with an odd number purple.

Can You See It?

Write the numbers you see with a . . .

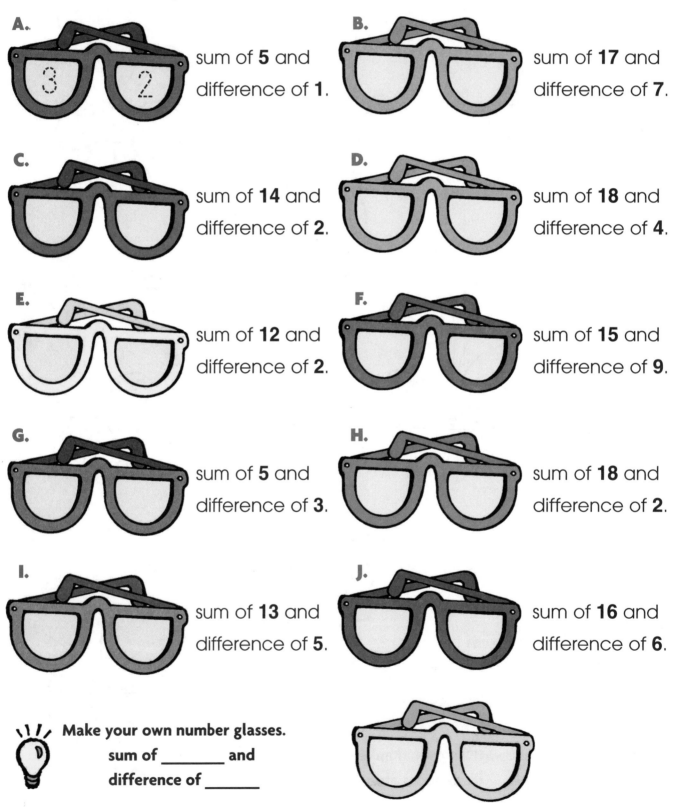

A. sum of **5** and difference of **1**.

B. sum of **17** and difference of **7**.

C. sum of **14** and difference of **2**.

D. sum of **18** and difference of **4**.

E. sum of **12** and difference of **2**.

F. sum of **15** and difference of **9**.

G. sum of **5** and difference of **3**.

H. sum of **18** and difference of **2**.

I. sum of **13** and difference of **5**.

J. sum of **16** and difference of **6**.

Make your own number glasses.
sum of _____ and
difference of _____

Planet Earth

Add.

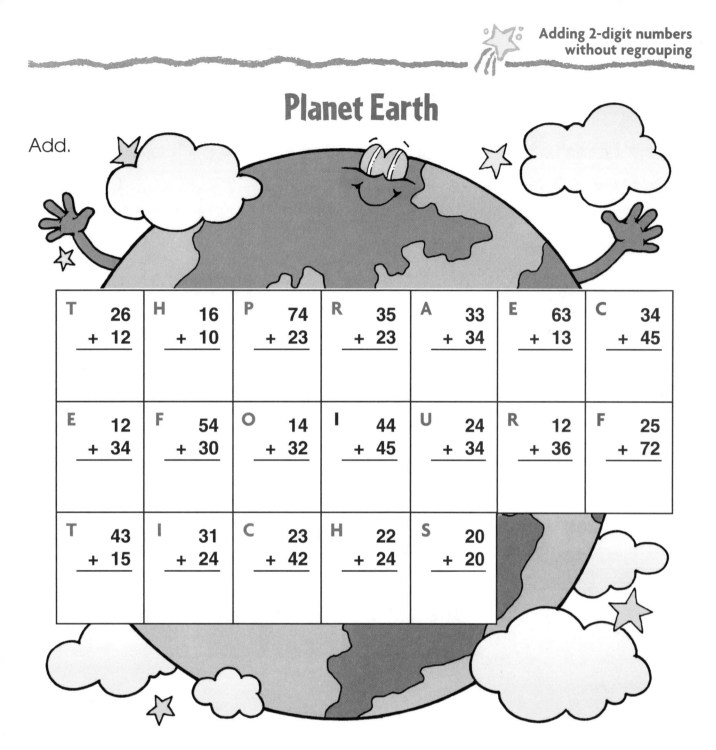

T 26 + 12	H 16 + 10	P 74 + 23	R 35 + 23	A 33 + 34	E 63 + 13	C 34 + 45
E 12 + 34	F 54 + 30	O 14 + 32	I 44 + 45	U 24 + 34	R 12 + 36	F 25 + 72
T 43 + 15	I 31 + 24	C 23 + 42	H 22 + 24	S 20 + 20		

For each sum that is an even number, write its letter below in order.

How much of the earth is covered by water?

___ ___ ___ ___ ___ — ___ ___ ___ ___ ___ ___

For each sum that is an odd number, write its letter below in order.

What is the biggest ocean?

___ ___ ___ ___ ___ ___ ___

Shape Tricks

Danny's class was learning about shapes. He noticed that you could draw a line across one shape to make two shapes. Draw a line through each shape below to make two new shapes. (Pattern blocks may help you.)

1. Make a square and a triangle.

2. Make two triangles.

3. Make two rectangles.

4. Make a triangle and a diamond.

5. Cut this twice to make 3 triangles.

Shape Study

A heptagon has 7 sides.

Connect the dots in the geoboards below to make other shapes with 7 sides.

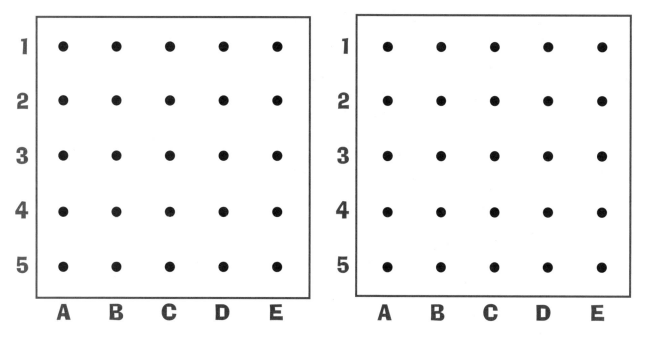

Shape Gaper

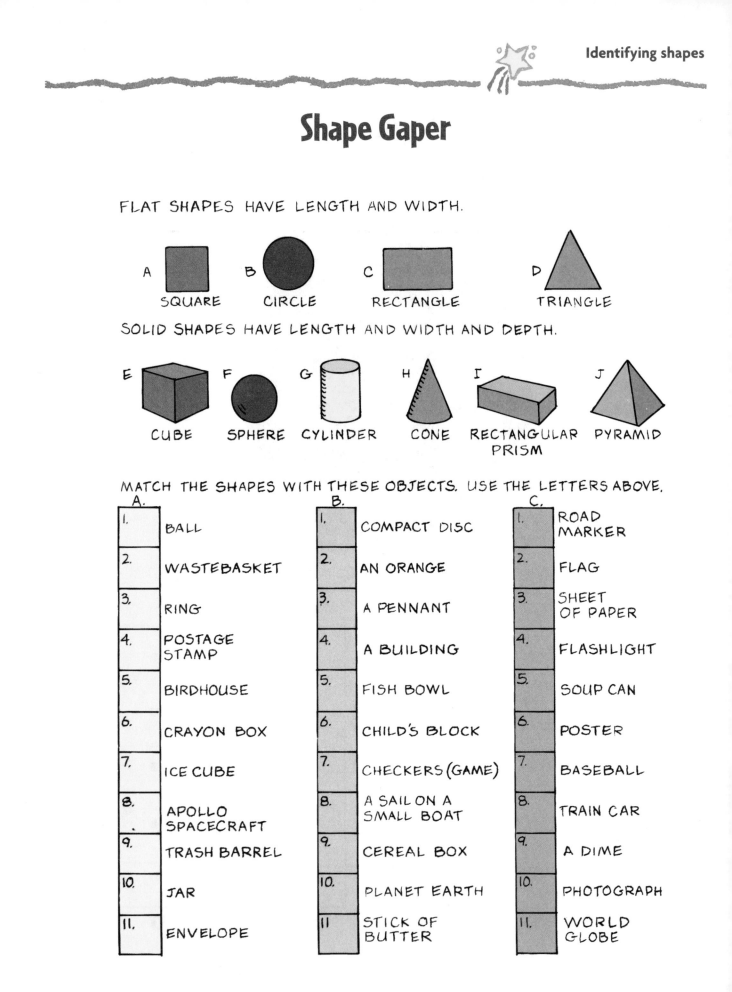

FLAT SHAPES HAVE LENGTH AND WIDTH.

A SQUARE
B CIRCLE
C RECTANGLE
D TRIANGLE

SOLID SHAPES HAVE LENGTH AND WIDTH AND DEPTH.

E CUBE
F SPHERE
G CYLINDER
H CONE
I RECTANGULAR PRISM
J PYRAMID

MATCH THE SHAPES WITH THESE OBJECTS. USE THE LETTERS ABOVE.

A.
1. BALL
2. WASTEBASKET
3. RING
4. POSTAGE STAMP
5. BIRDHOUSE
6. CRAYON BOX
7. ICE CUBE
8. APOLLO SPACECRAFT
9. TRASH BARREL
10. JAR
11. ENVELOPE

B.
1. COMPACT DISC
2. AN ORANGE
3. A PENNANT
4. A BUILDING
5. FISH BOWL
6. CHILD'S BLOCK
7. CHECKERS (GAME)
8. A SAIL ON A SMALL BOAT
9. CEREAL BOX
10. PLANET EARTH
11. STICK OF BUTTER

C.
1. ROAD MARKER
2. FLAG
3. SHEET OF PAPER
4. FLASHLIGHT
5. SOUP CAN
6. POSTER
7. BASEBALL
8. TRAIN CAR
9. A DIME
10. PHOTOGRAPH
11. WORLD GLOBE

Riddle Fun

What wears shoes, sandals, and boots, but has no feet?

A ___ ___ ___ ___ ___ ___ ___ ___

To find out, write each number in standard form. Then look for the numbers in the puzzle and circle them. They are written up, down, forward, and backward. When you have circled all the numbers given, the letters in the blocks left uncircled spell the answer to the riddle. The first number has been circled for you.

4 B	3 A	2 R	1 K	9 S	9 I	5 G
8 R	1 M	7 Y	1 S	7 O	0 D	6 T
8 D	5 W	1 E	8 T	9 E	1 S	4 S
1 W	6 P	2 C	5 X	3 A	3 Z	9 P
4 L	9 J	7 F	7 S	0 R	7 M	0 L
8 H	3 F	6 Y	9 K	2 T	0 E	9 Q

8 ones
1 ten   = [518]
5 hundreds

5 ones
1 ten   = [   ]
3 hundreds

6 ones
7 tens   = [   ]
2 hundreds

3 ones
9 tens   = [   ]
6 hundreds

7 ones
3 tens   = [   ]
1 hundred

4 ones
6 tens   = [   ]
5 hundreds

9 ones
0 tens   = [   ]
9 hundreds

1 one
1 ten   = [   ]
8 hundreds

9 ones
0 tens   = [   ]
2 hundreds

7 ones
1 ten   = [   ]
7 hundreds

6 ones
3 tens   = [   ]
8 hundreds

1 one
2 tens   = [   ]
3 hundreds

8 ones
8 tens   = [   ]
4 hundreds

7 ones
5 tens   = [   ]
8 hundreds

2 ones
3 tens   = [   ]
4 hundreds

7 ones
0 tens   = [   ]
7 hundreds

Detective Work

Use the code to help Detective Dave discover the secret phone number.
The first problem has been done for you.

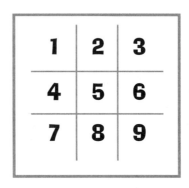

1	2	3
4	5	6
7	8	9

1.

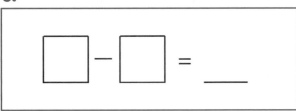

$7 - 1 = 6$

2.

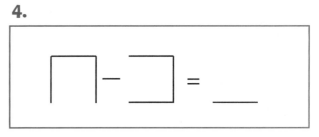

$\_ - \_ = \_$

3.

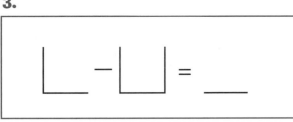

$\_ - \_ = \_$

4.

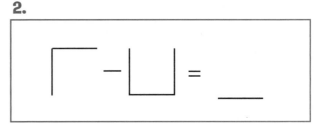

$\_ - \_ = \_$

5.

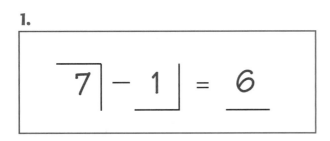

$\_ - \_ = \_$

6.

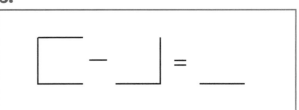

$\_ - \_ = \_$

7.

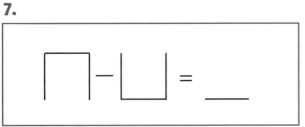

$\_ - \_ = \_$

The phone number is:

_ _ _ - _ _ _ _

Weather Drops

Subtract. Using the difference in each raindrop, write the weather words in order of their differences from least to greatest by the umbrella handle. Then color your favorite kind of "weather drop" blue.

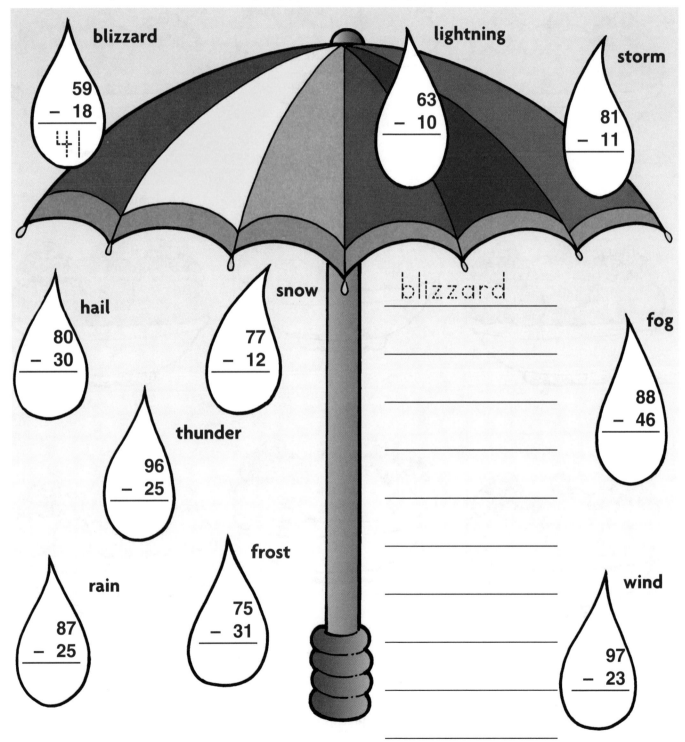

blizzard

$\begin{array}{r} 59 \\ -\ 18 \\ \hline 41 \end{array}$

lightning

$\begin{array}{r} 63 \\ -\ 10 \\ \hline \end{array}$

storm

$\begin{array}{r} 81 \\ -\ 11 \\ \hline \end{array}$

hail

$\begin{array}{r} 80 \\ -\ 30 \\ \hline \end{array}$

snow

$\begin{array}{r} 77 \\ -\ 12 \\ \hline \end{array}$

blizzard

fog

$\begin{array}{r} 88 \\ -\ 46 \\ \hline \end{array}$

thunder

$\begin{array}{r} 96 \\ -\ 25 \\ \hline \end{array}$

frost

$\begin{array}{r} 75 \\ -\ 31 \\ \hline \end{array}$

rain

$\begin{array}{r} 87 \\ -\ 25 \\ \hline \end{array}$

wind

$\begin{array}{r} 97 \\ -\ 23 \\ \hline \end{array}$

Triple the Fun

Add. Write the sum on each bowl.

Color bowls with 1, 5, or 8 in the ones place yellow.
Color bowls with 0, 4, or 7 in the ones place pink.
Color bowls with 2, 6, or 9 in the ones place brown.

Measuring Perimeter

Use the inch side of a ruler and measure each side of each triangle. Write the inches in the spaces below. Then add up all the sides to find the perimeter, or distance around each triangle.

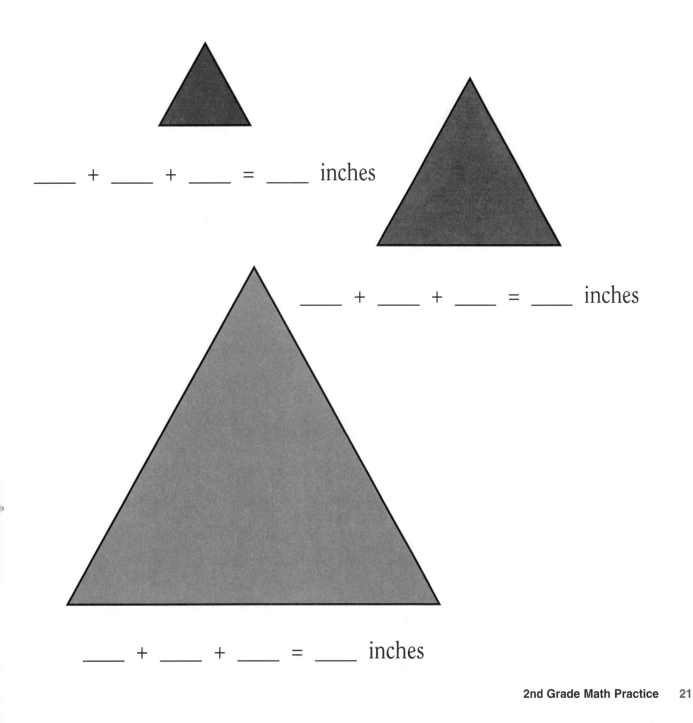

_____ + _____ + _____ = _____ inches

_____ + _____ + _____ = _____ inches

_____ + _____ + _____ = _____ inches

Best Estimator

LENGTH CAN BE MEASURED IN INCHES (IN.), FEET (FT.), YARDS (YD.),
AND MILES (MI.). 12 IN. = 1 FT. 5280 FT. = 1 MILE.

UNDERLINE THE MORE SENSIBLE MEASURE.

How many inches to Boston, Sir?

BUS STOP

1. HEIGHT OF A BOOKCASE
    INCHES   FEET

2. WIDTH OF YOUR BACKYARD
    YARDS   MILES

3. LENGTH OF A RIVER
    MILES   YARDS

4. WIDTH OF A DESK
    INCHES   FEET

5. LENGTH OF YOUR ARM
    FEET   INCHES

6. LENGTH OF A COMB
    INCHES   FEET

7. LENGTH OF A FOOTBALL FIELD
    INCHES   YARDS

8. DISTANCE FROM EARTH TO MOON
    MILES   YARDS

9. DEPTH OF A SWIMMING POOL
    FEET   INCHES

10. LENGTH OF A
    TUBE OF TOOTHPASTE
    INCHES   FEET

11. HEIGHT OF A REFRIGERATOR
    INCHES   FEET

12. WIDTH OF A BEDROOM
    FEET   INCHES

13. DISTANCE BETWEEN 2 CITIES
    YARDS   MILES

14. LENGTH OF A DOLLAR
    INCHES   FEET

15. LENGTH OF AN AUTOMOBILE
    INCHES   FEET

Money Matters

Alex asked his little brother Billy to trade piggy banks.

Alex's bank has these coins: **Billy's has these coins:**

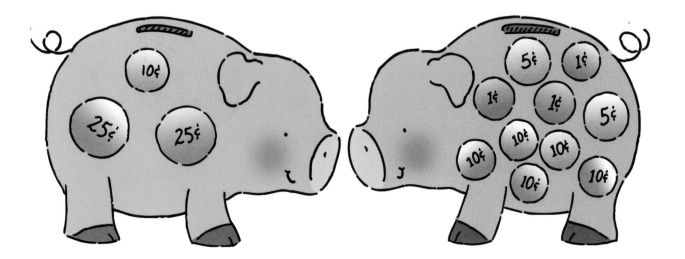

Do you think this is a fair trade? _____

Test your answer:

Add up Alex's coins: _____

Add up Billy's coins: _____

Write the totals in this Greater Than/Less Than equation:

_____ > _____

Who has more money? _____

Just Snacks

Use the menu on page 25 to answer the
following questions.

1. Which snack costs the most?

   _____

   How much do they cost?

   _____

2. Which sweet costs the least? _____

   How much does it cost? _____

3. Henry spends 50¢ on a snack.

   What does he buy? _____

4. Gina orders a drink. She spends 15¢.

   Which drink does she order? _____

5. Dan orders popcorn and a cookie.

   How much does he pay? _____

6. Pat buys a cup of soup and a sip of milk.

   How much does she spend? _____

Small Snacks

Potato Chips ....60¢

Pretzels ....45¢

Popcorn ....55¢

Peanuts ....50¢

Bagel Bites ....65¢

Teeny Sandwiches.......75¢

Cup of Soup ....40¢

Small Sweets
& Drinks

Cookie ....40¢

Donut Hole ....25¢

Ice Cream Bar ....60¢

Raisins ....30¢

Sip of Milk............10¢

Gulp of Juice..........15¢

Prime Timer

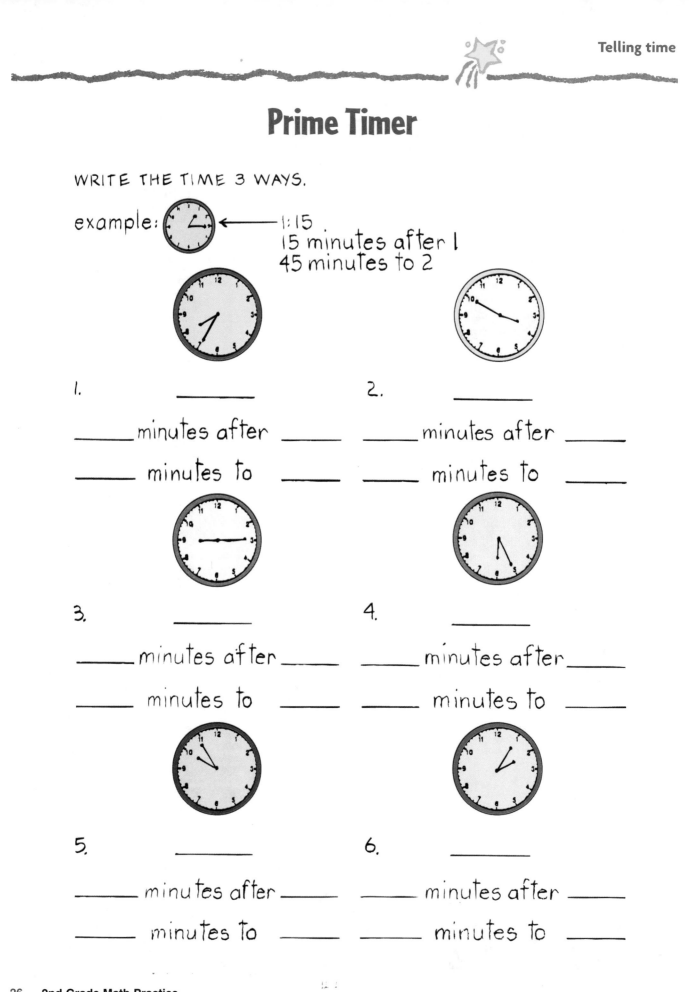

WRITE THE TIME 3 WAYS.

example: ←———— 1:15
15 minutes after 1
45 minutes to 2

1. _____

_____ minutes after _____

_____ minutes to _____

2. _____

_____ minutes after _____

_____ minutes to _____

3. _____

_____ minutes after _____

_____ minutes to _____

4. _____

_____ minutes after _____

_____ minutes to _____

5. _____

_____ minutes after _____

_____ minutes to _____

6. _____

_____ minutes after _____

_____ minutes to _____

Day by Day

Color each special date on the calendar.

July

Sun.	Mon.	Tues.	Wed.	Thur.	Fri.	Sat.
		1	2	3	4	5
6	7	8	9	10	11	12
13	14	15	16	17	18	19
20	21	22	23	24	25	26
27	28	29	30	31		

A. Camp begins one week after the second Monday. Color this date red.

B. The baseball game is two weeks before the fourth Wednesday. Color this date green.

C. The birthday party is two weeks after the second Saturday. Color this date purple.

D. The swim meet is three weeks before the fifth Tuesday. Color this date blue.

E. The trip to the zoo is one week before the third Sunday. Color this date orange.

F. The picnic is two weeks before the fifth Thursday. Color this date yellow.

G. What date is 14 days after the third Wednesday? Color this date pink.

H. What date is 18 days before the fourth Friday? Color this date brown.

Crack the Numbers

Look at the number on each chick. Write the number of tens and ones on the egg. Then trade one ten for ten ones.

35
3 tens   5 ones
2 tens
15 ones

47
___ tens   ___ ones
___ tens
___ ones

82
___ tens   ___ ones
___ tens
___ ones

94
___ tens   ___ ones
___ tens
___ ones

61
___ tens   ___ ones
___ tens
___ ones

90
___ tens   ___ ones
___ tens
___ ones

Kaleidoscope

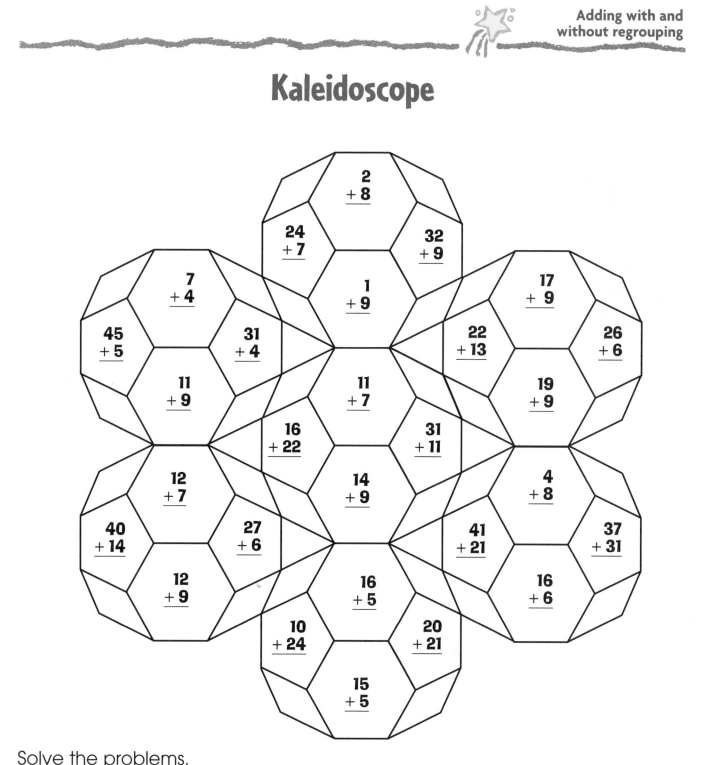

Solve the problems.

If the answer is between 1 and 30, color the shape red.

If the answer is between 31 and 99, color the shape gray.

Finish by coloring the other shapes with the colors of your choice.

Extra: Name two numbers that when added together equal 27.

_____ + _____ = _____   _____ + _____ = _____

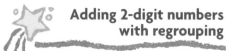

Treasure of a Book

Add. Then color each box with an odd sum to help the boy find his way to the book. Hint: Remember to look in the ones place.

	47 + 24	74 + 19	78 + 12	15 + 37
48 + 44	31 + 59	52 + 39	29 + 57	73 + 19
63 + 18	14 + 67	57 + 16	24 + 18	63 + 29
57 + 28	27 + 47	76 + 16	72 + 18	76 + 18
32 + 19	17 + 24	55 + 38	32 + 49	

How Do We Get There?

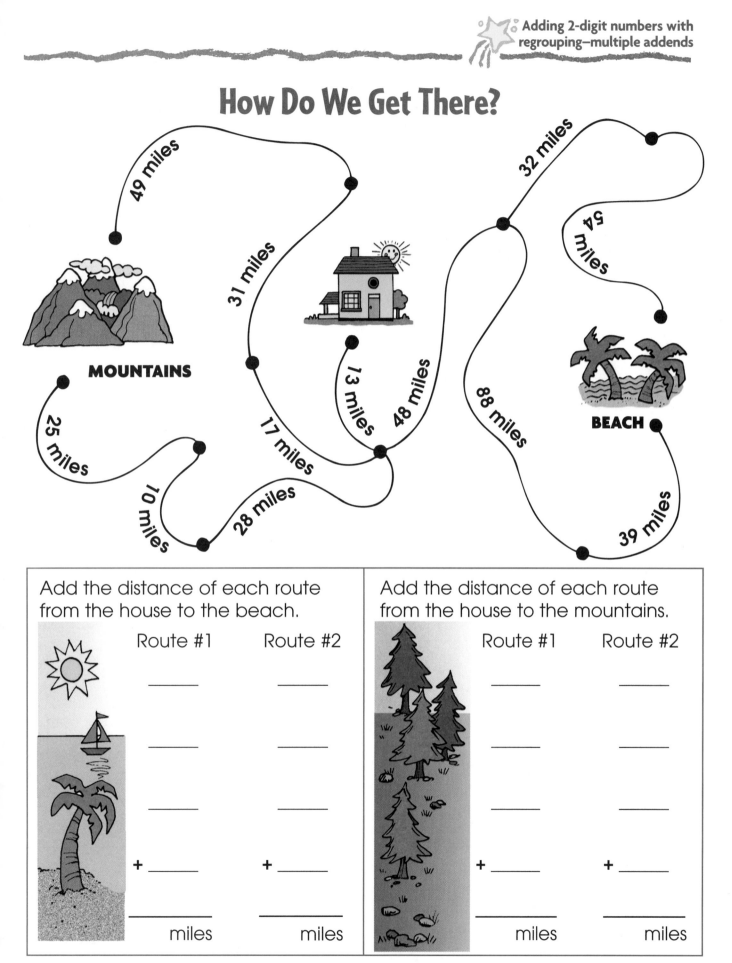

49 miles

32 miles

31 miles

54 miles

MOUNTAINS

13 miles

48 miles

88 miles

BEACH

25 miles

17 miles

10 miles

28 miles

39 miles

Add the distance of each route from the house to the beach.

Route #1   Route #2

_____   _____

_____   _____

_____   _____

+ _____   + _____

_____   _____

miles   miles

Add the distance of each route from the house to the mountains.

Route #1   Route #2

_____   _____

_____   _____

_____   _____

+ _____   + _____

_____   _____

miles   miles

First, Next, Last

Subtract. Then number the pictures in order from least to greatest.

A.

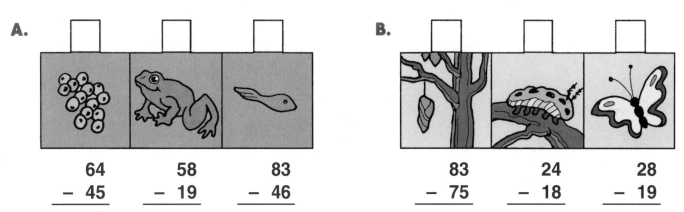

| 64 | 58 | 83 |
| - 45 | - 19 | - 46 |

B.

| 83 | 24 | 28 |
| - 75 | - 18 | - 19 |

C.

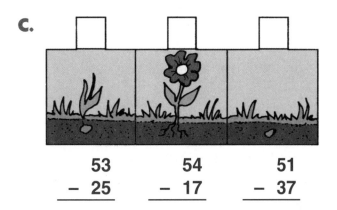

| 53 | 54 | 51 |
| - 25 | - 17 | - 37 |

D.

| 88 | 91 | 82 |
| - 59 | - 53 | - 45 |

E.

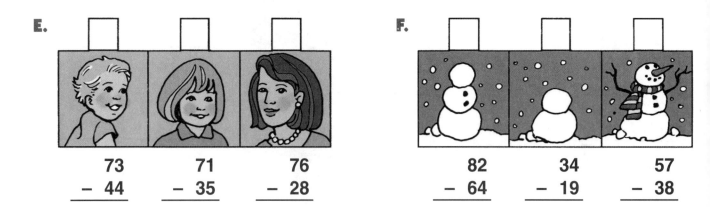

| 73 | 71 | 76 |
| - 44 | - 35 | - 28 |

F.

| 82 | 34 | 57 |
| - 64 | - 19 | - 38 |

Teenie Tiny Babies

Add or subtract.

U. 42
  + 39

L. 53
  − 48

N. 31
  + 29

C. 74
  − 28

O. 44
  + 46

P. 75
  − 37

H. 40
  − 17

K. 27
  + 36

S. 96
  − 48

A. 62
  − 48

G. 80
  − 62

M. 55
  + 16

R. 88
  − 19

Write the letter that goes with each number.

I am smaller than your
thumb when I'm born.
____ ____ ____ ____ ____ ____ ____ ____
63   14   60   18   14   69   90   90

I am even smaller.
____ ____ ____ ____ ____
63   90   14   5   14

I am smaller than a bumblebee.
____ ____ ____ ____ ____ ____ ____
90   38   90   48   48   81   71

Since we are so little, we
live right next to our mothers in a safe, warm ____ ____ ____ ____ ____ .
38   90   81   46   23

December Weather

In December, Mrs. Monroe's class drew the weather on a calendar. Each kind of weather has a picture:

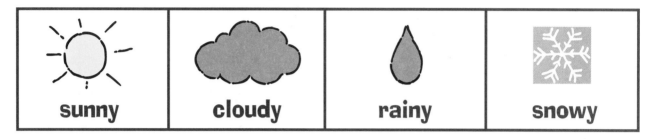

| sunny | cloudy | rainy | snowy |

Look at the calendar. Answer the questions below.

How many sunny days did they have? _____

How many cloudy days did they have? _____

How many rainy days did they have? _____

How many snowy days did they have? _____

Which kind of weather did they have the most? _____

Great Graphing

The picture was made with 7 different shapes. How many of each shape was used? Color in the shapes, following the instructions. Then color in the boxes on the chart, 1 box for each shape used.

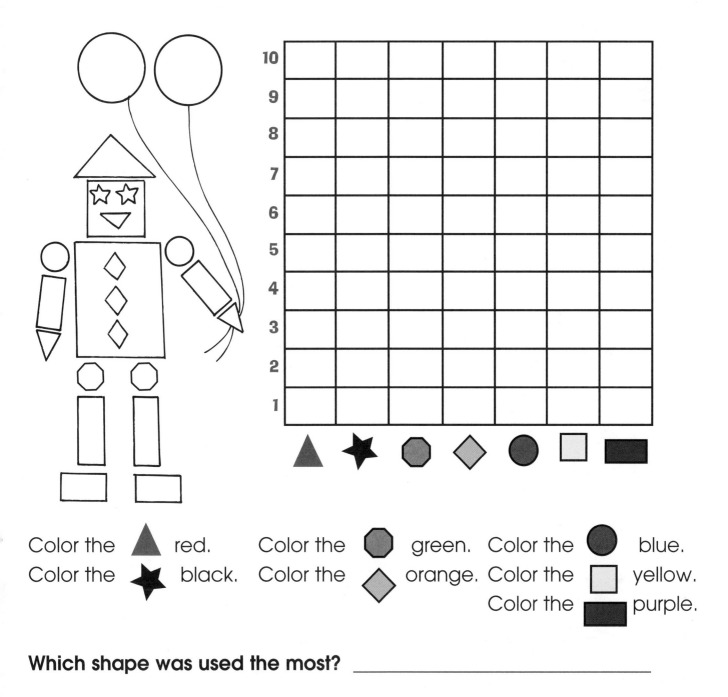

Color the ▲ red.   Color the ⬣ green.   Color the ● blue.
Color the ★ black.   Color the ◆ orange.   Color the ▢ yellow.
                                              Color the ▬ purple.

Which shape was used the most? _____

Pizza Vote

Use the circle graph to compare the
results of the pizza vote.

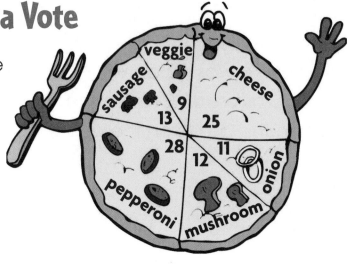

A. How many students voted for
pepperoni and cheese in all?

B. How many more students
voted for cheese than veggie?

C. How many more students
voted for pepperoni than
sausage?

D. How many students voted for
mushroom and veggie
altogether?

E. How many more students
voted for mushroom than
veggie?

F. How many students voted for
sausage and pepperoni in all?

G. How many students voted for
veggie, cheese, and mushroom
in all?

 **Find the total number of students who voted.**

Hundreds of Pumpkins

Regroup tens into hundreds. Remember: 10 tens = 1 hundred. Write the
number of hundreds and the number of remaining tens.

27 tens
_2_ hundreds
_7_ tens

84 tens
_____ hundreds
_____ tens

93 tens
_____ hundreds
_____ tens

71 tens
_____ hundreds
_____ tens

56 tens
_____ hundreds
_____ tens

32 tens
_____ hundreds
_____ tens

49 tens
_____ hundreds
_____ tens

65 tens
_____ hundreds
_____ tens

Write the number.

5 hundreds **7 tens** **0 ones**

8 hundreds **0 tens** **4 ones**

Eager Leader

Powerful Presidents

Add. Color each even sum red to learn about George Washington. Color each odd sum blue to learn about Abe Lincoln. Hint: Look in the ones place.

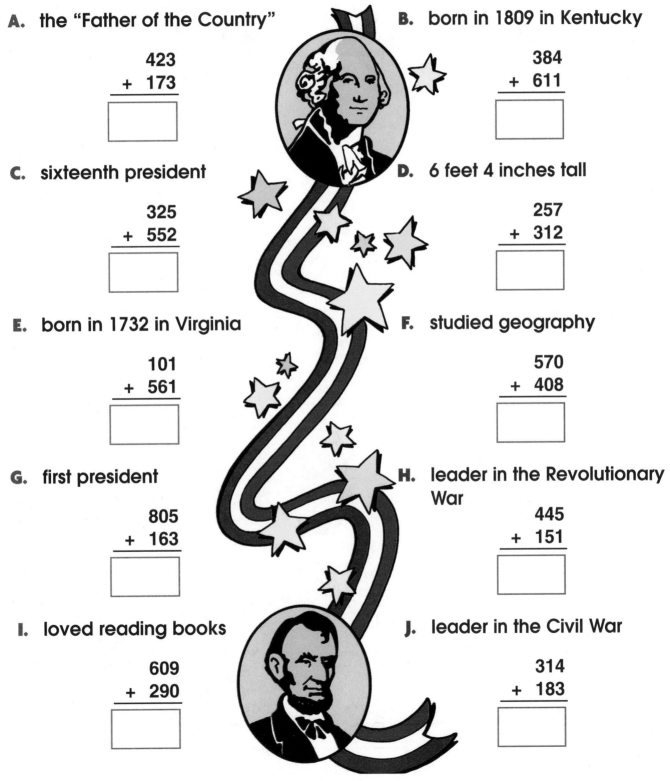

A. the "Father of the Country"

```
  423
+ 173
```

B. born in 1809 in Kentucky

```
  384
+ 611
```

C. sixteenth president

```
  325
+ 552
```

D. 6 feet 4 inches tall

```
  257
+ 312
```

E. born in 1732 in Virginia

```
  101
+ 561
```

F. studied geography

```
  570
+ 408
```

G. first president

```
  805
+ 163
```

H. leader in the Revolutionary War

```
  445
+ 151
```

I. loved reading books

```
  609
+ 290
```

J. leader in the Civil War

```
  314
+ 183
```

Through the Tunnels

Add. Then trace the mole's path to the top. The mole must travel through tunnels with a zero in the sum.

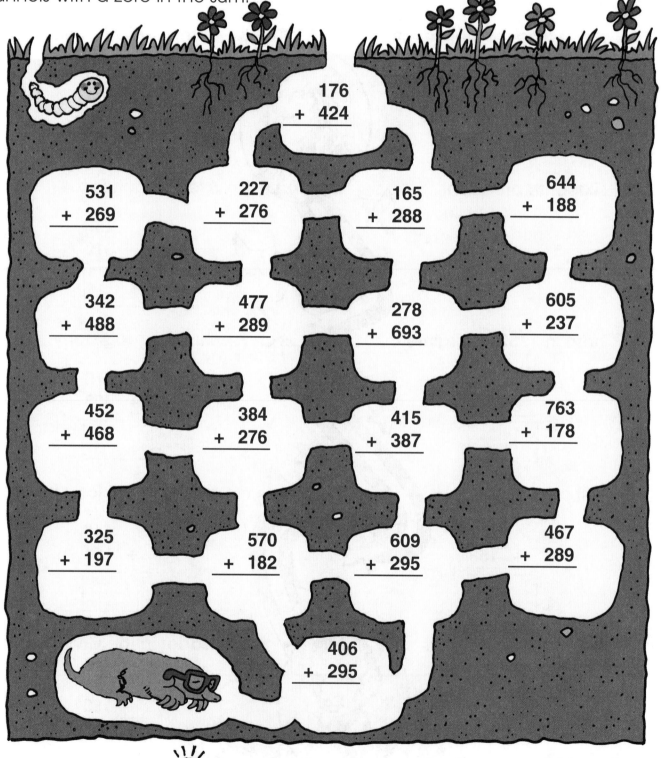

176
+ 424

531
+ 269

227
+ 276

165
+ 288

644
+ 188

342
+ 488

477
+ 289

278
+ 693

605
+ 237

452
+ 468

384
+ 276

415
+ 387

763
+ 178

325
+ 197

570
+ 182

609
+ 295

467
+ 289

406
+ 295

 On another piece of paper, write three more problems that have a zero in the sum.

Scholastic Teaching Resources

The Sun's Family

Draw a line to each matching difference to connect each planet to a fact about it.

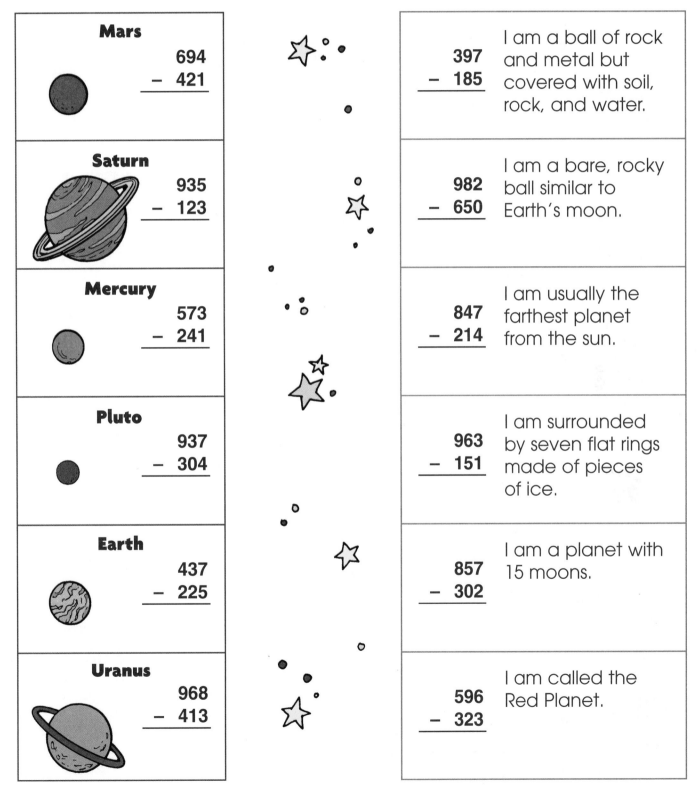

Mars

694
− 421

Saturn

935
− 123

Mercury

573
− 241

Pluto

937
− 304

Earth

437
− 225

Uranus

968
− 413

397
− 185   I am a ball of rock and metal but covered with soil, rock, and water.

982
− 650   I am a bare, rocky ball similar to Earth's moon.

847
− 214   I am usually the farthest planet from the sun.

963
− 151   I am surrounded by seven flat rings made of pieces of ice.

857
− 302   I am a planet with 15 moons.

596
− 323   I am called the Red Planet.

A Place in Space

Draw a line to each matching difference to connect each planet or space object to a fact about it.

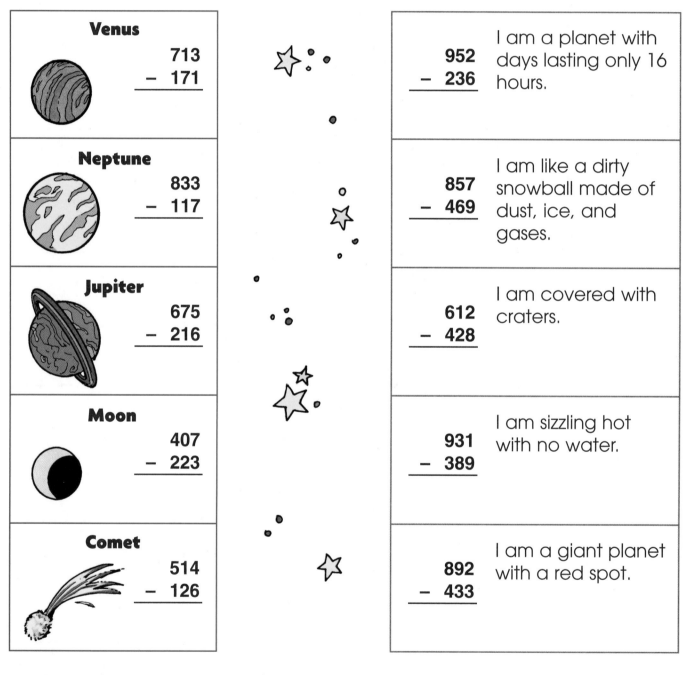

Venus
713
− 171

Neptune
833
− 117

Jupiter
675
− 216

Moon
407
− 223

Comet
514
− 126

952
− 236
I am a planet with days lasting only 16 hours.

857
− 469
I am like a dirty snowball made of dust, ice, and gases.

612
− 428
I am covered with craters.

931
− 389
I am sizzling hot with no water.

892
− 433
I am a giant planet with a red spot.

Complete each pattern. Then tell someone the pattern for each set of numbers.

900, 800, 700, _____, _____, _____, _____, _____, _____

900, 700, 500, _____, _____

800, 600, 400, _____

Chester's Cakes and Pies

Fill in the blanks. Chester Chipmunk was cutting cakes and pies.
Bobby Bear said, "Some aren't cut in half. When you cut something in
half, there are _____ pieces and both of the pieces are the
same _____."
Here is how Chester cut the cakes and pies.
Circle the desserts that are cut in half correctly.

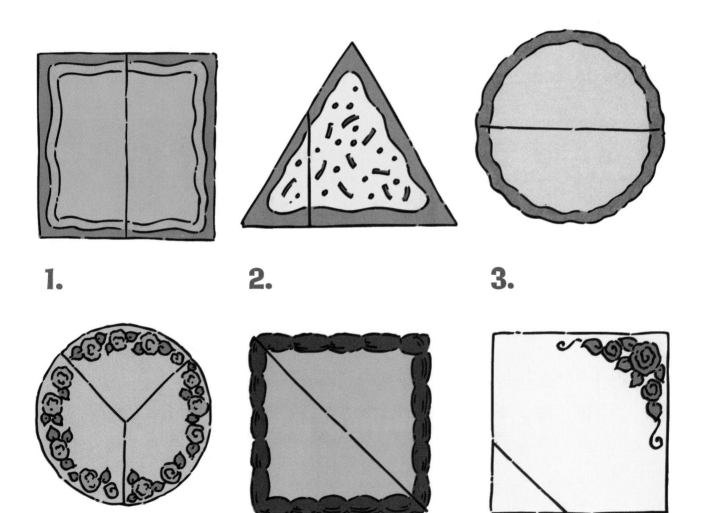

1.   2.   3.

4.   5.   6.

Fraction Fun

Something that is split in 2 equal parts is divided in "half."

These two shapes are divided in half.

A fraction has a number on the top: ⟶ 1

A fraction has a number on the bottom, too: ⟶ 2

The top number tells the "fraction," or parts, of the whole.

The bottom number tells the number of parts in the whole.

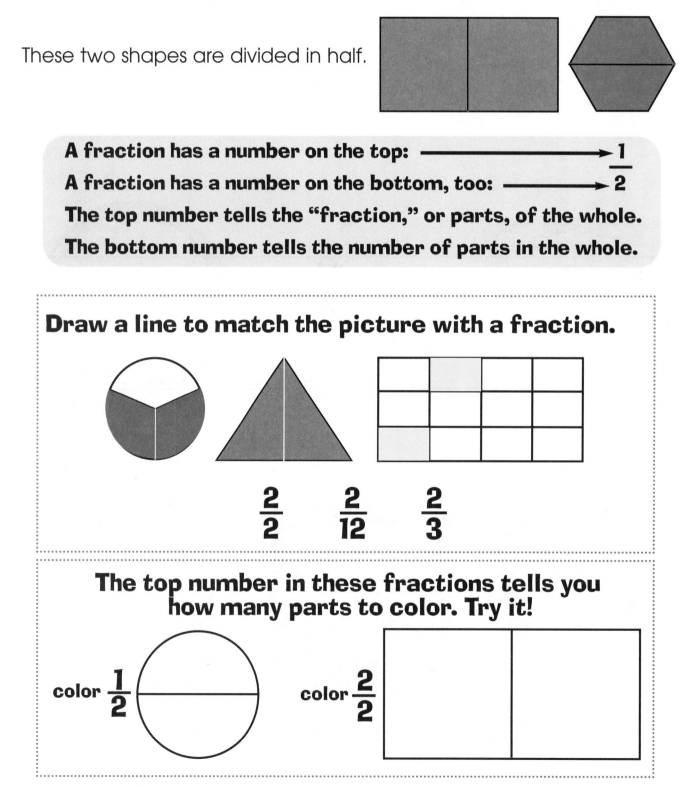

Draw a line to match the picture with a fraction.

$$\frac{2}{2} \qquad \frac{2}{12} \qquad \frac{2}{3}$$

The top number in these fractions tells you how many parts to color. Try it!

color $\frac{1}{2}$ color $\frac{2}{2}$

Fun With Fractions

A fraction has two numbers. The top number will tell you how many parts to color. The bottom number tells you how many parts there are.

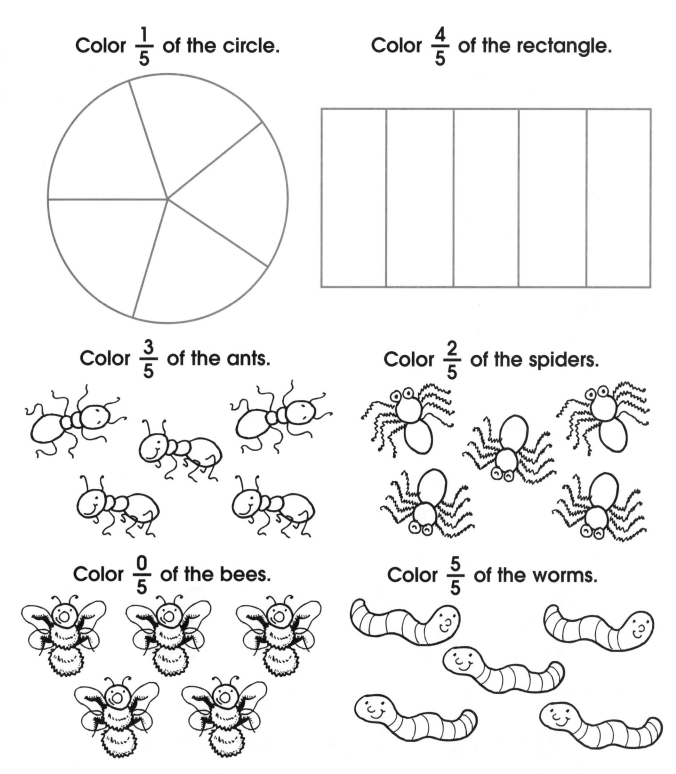

Color $\frac{1}{5}$ of the circle.

Color $\frac{4}{5}$ of the rectangle.

Color $\frac{3}{5}$ of the ants.

Color $\frac{2}{5}$ of the spiders.

Color $\frac{0}{5}$ of the bees.

Color $\frac{5}{5}$ of the worms.

More Fun With Fractions

A fraction has two numbers. The top number will tell you how many parts to color. The bottom number tells you how many total parts there are.

$\frac{10}{10}$ is the whole circle.

$\frac{10}{10}$ is the whole rectangle.

Color $\frac{8}{10}$ of the circle.

Color $\frac{4}{10}$ of the rectangle.

How much is not colored? ____

How much is not colored? ____

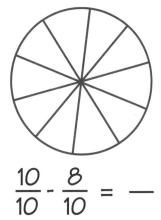

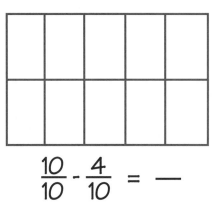

$$\frac{10}{10} - \frac{8}{10} = —$$

$$\frac{10}{10} - \frac{4}{10} = —$$

Solve this fraction equation. Cross out the dogs to help you.

$$\frac{10}{10} - \frac{3}{10} = —$$

Answer Key

Page 5
1. 67; 2. 34, 35; 3. 42, 43;
4. 16, 18; 5. 73, 74, 75; 6. 31, 32;
7. 10, 12, 14, 16; 8. 15, 18, 21, 24;
9. 83, 84, 85, 86, 87, 88; 10. after;
11. before; 12. after; 13. before;
14. before; 15. before

Page 6
1. 32, 42, 52, 62, 72, 82, 92; 2. 70, 60,
50, 40, 30, 20, 10; 3. 67, 57, 47, 37,
27, 17, 7; 4. 44, 55, 66, 77, 88, 99

Page 7
1. 11 < 21; 2. 56 < 72; 3. 47 = 47;
4. 64 >10 5. 59 = 59; 6. 38 > 17;
7. 526 < 527; 8. 159 > 42; 9–16.
Answers will vary. 17. 73 61 54 37;
18. 96 43 24 22; 19. 79 78 69 51;
20. 51 37 27 15

Page 8
Answers will vary.

Page 9
15; 8

Page 10

seven; nine

Page 11
Check that the child has drawn the
correct number of petals on each
flower. Bows with 4, 6, 8, and 10
should be colored yellow. Bows with 3,
5, 7, and 9 should be colored purple.

Page 12
A. 3, 2; B. 12, 5; C. 8, 6; D. 11, 7;
E. 7, 5; F. 12, 3; G. 4, 1; H. 10, 8; I. 9, 4;
J. 11, 5; Answers will vary.

Page 13
38, 26, 97, 58, 67, 76, 79; 46, 84, 46,
89, 58, 48, 97; 58, 55, 65, 46, 40;
THREE-FOURTHS, PACIFIC

Page 14
1. ⌂ 2. ◺ 3. ▭ or ▭ 4. ◿ 5. ◹

This line
could move
up or down.

This line
could move
left or right.

Page 15
Answers will vary.

Page 16
A. 1F, 2G, 3B, 4C or A, 5E, 6I, 7E, 8H,
9G, 10G, 11C; B. 1B, 2F, 3D, 4I, 5F,
6E, 7A, 8D, 9I, 10F, 11I; C. 1H, 2C, 3C,
4G, 5G, 6C, 7F, 8I, 9B, 10C or A, 11F

Page 17
A sidewalk. 518, 315, 276, 693, 137,
564, 909, 811, 209, 717, 836, 321,
488, 857, 432, 707

Page 18
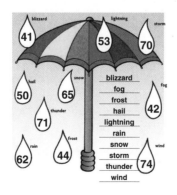

1. 7 − 1 = 6; 2. 9 − 2 = 7;
3. 3 − 2 = 1; 4. 8 − 4 = 4;
5. 5 − 5 = 0; 6. 6 − 1 = 5;
7. 8 − 2 = 6
The phone number is 671-4056.

Page 19

Page 20
10, 12, 16; 18, 14, 19; 15, 11, 17;
Bowls with 11, 15, and 18 should be
colored yellow. Bowls with 10, 14, and
17 should be colored pink. Bowls with
12, 16, and 19 should be colored
brown.

Page 21
1 + 1 + 1 = 3 inches; 2 + 2 + 2 = 6
inches; 4 + 4 + 4 = 12 inches

Page 22
1. feet; 2. yards; 3. miles; 4. inches;
5. inches; 6. inches; 7. yards; 8. miles;
9. feet; 10. inches; 11. feet; 12. feet;
13. miles; 14. inches; 15. feet

Page 23
Alex's coins: 25¢ + 25¢ + 10¢ = 60¢
Billy's coins: 10¢ + 10¢ + 10¢ + 10¢ +
10¢ + 5¢ + 5¢ + 1¢ + 1¢ + 1¢ = 63¢
63¢ > 60¢ Billy has more money.

Pages 24–25
1. Teeny Sandwiches; 75¢; 2. Donut
Hole; 25¢; 3. Peanuts; 4. Gulp of Juice;
5. 95¢; 6. 50¢

Page 26
1. 7:35, 35 minutes after 7, 25 minutes
to 8; 2. 3:50, 50 minutes after 3, 10
minutes to 4; 3. 9:15, 15 minutes after
9, 45 minutes to 10; 4. 6:25, 25
minutes after 6, 35 minutes to 7;
5. 9:55, 55 minutes after 9, 5 minutes
to 10; 6. 2:05, 5 minutes after 2, 55
minutes to 3

Page 27
Check that the child has colored the
appropriate spaces. A. 21; B. 9;
C. 26; D. 8; E. 13; F. 17; G. 30; H. 7

Page 28
35: 3 tens 5 ones, 2 tens 15 ones;
47: 4 tens 7 ones, 3 tens 17 ones;
82: 8 tens 2 ones, 7 tens 12 ones;
94: 9 tens 4 ones, 8 tens 14 ones;
61: 6 tens 1 one, 5 tens 11 ones;
90: 9 tens 0 ones, 8 tens 10 ones

Page 29

2 + 8 = 10; 24 + 7 = 31; 32 + 9 = 41;
1 + 9 = 10; 7 + 4 = 11; 45 + 5 = 50;
31 + 4 = 35; 11 + 9 = 20; 17 + 9 = 26;
22 + 13 = 35; 26 + 6 = 32; 19 + 9 =
28; 11 + 7 = 18; 16 + 22 = 38; 31 +
11 = 42; 14 + 9 = 23; 12 + 7 = 19;
40 + 14 = 54; 27 + 6 = 33; 12 + 9 = 21;
4 + 8 = 12; 41 + 21 = 62; 37 + 31 =
68; 16 + 6 = 22; 16 + 5 = 21; 10 + 24
= 34; 20 + 21 = 41; 15 + 5 = 20
Extra: Answers will vary.

Page 30

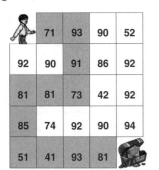

Page 31

Beach: Route #1—13 + 48 + 32 + 54
= 147 miles; Route #2—13 + 48 + 88
+ 39 = 188 miles

Mountains: Route #1—13 + 17 + 31 +
49 = 110 miles; Route #2—13 + 28 +
10 + 25 = 76 miles

Page 32

A. 19, 39, 37; 1, 3, 2; B. 8, 6, 9; 2, 1,
3; C. 28, 37, 14; 2, 3, 1; D. 29, 38, 37;
1, 3, 2; E. 29, 36, 48; 1, 2, 3;
F. 18, 15, 19; 2, 1, 3

Page 33

U. 81; L. 5; N. 60; C. 46; O. 90; P. 38;
H. 23; K. 63; S. 48; A. 14; G. 18; M.
71; R. 69; KANGAROO; KOALA;
OPOSSUM; POUCH

Page 34

Sunny days: 12; Cloudy days: 8; Rainy
days: 5; Snowy days: 6; Sunny

Page 35

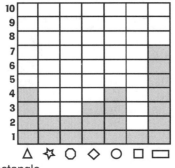

Rectangle

Page 36

A. 28 + 25 = 53; B. 25 − 9 = 16;
C. 28 − 13 = 15; D. 12 + 9 = 21;
E. 12 − 9 = 3; F. 13 + 28 = 41;
G. 9 + 25 + 12 = 46; 98 students

Page 37

2 hundreds 7 tens,
8 hundreds 4 tens,
9 hundreds 3 tens,
7 hundreds 1 ten;
5 hundreds 6 tens,
3 hundreds 2 tens,
4 hundreds 9 tens,
6 hundreds 5 tens; 570; 804

Page 38

Page 39

A. 596, red; B. 995, blue; C. 877, blue;
D. 569, blue; E. 662, red; F. 978, red;
G. 968, red; H. 596, red; I. 899, blue;
J. 497, blue

Page 40

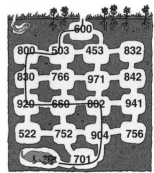

Page 41

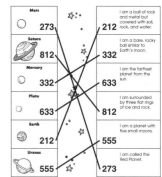

Page 42

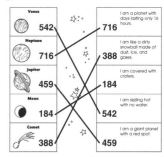

600, 500, 400, 300, 200, 100, subtract
100; 300, 100, subtract 200; 200,
subtract 200.

Page 43

2, size; Correct pies: 1, 3, 5

Page 44

2/2 matches triangle, 2/3 matches
circle, 2/12 matches rectangle; color
1/2 circle, color the whole rectangle

Page 45

1/5 of the circle, 4/5 of the rectangle,
3 ants, 2 spiders, 0 bees, 5 worms

Page 46

2/10, 6/10, 7/10